THE SCIENCE OF

ELECTRICITY & MAGNETISM

PROJECTS AND EXPERIMENTS WITH ELECTRONS AND MAGNETS

TABLETOP SCIENTIST – ELECTRICITY & MAGNETISM
was produced by

David West 👫 **Children's Books**
7 Princeton Court
55 Felsham Road
London SW15 1AZ

Designer: David West
Editor: Gail Bushnell
Picture Research: Gail Bushnell

First published in Great Britain by Heinemann
Library, Halley Court, Jordan Hill, Oxford
OX2 8EJ, part of Harcourt Education.
Heinemann is a registered trademark
of Harcourt Education Ltd.

09 08 07 06 05
10 9 8 7 6 5 4 3 2 1

ISBN 0 431 01334 9 (HB)
ISBN 0 431 01340 3 (PB)

British Library Cataloguing in Publication Data

Parker, Steve
The science of electricity and magnetism. - (Tabletop
scientist)
1. Electricity - Juvenile literature 2. Magnetism -
Juvenile literature
I. Title
537

Printed and bound in China

PHOTO CREDITS :
Abbreviations: t-top, m-middle, b-bottom, r-right,
l-left, c-centre.

Pages 4t, 10, 12 – Corbis Images. 8t (Roger-Viollet);
18–19 (Sipa Press); 22–23 – Rex Features Ltd.

Every effort has been made to contact copyright
holders of any material reproduced in this book.
Any omissions will be rectified in subsequent
printings if notice is given to the publishers.

With special thanks to the models: Meshach Burton,
Sam Heming De-Allie, Annabel Garnham, Andrew
Gregson, Hannah Holmes, Molly Rose Ibbett,
Margaux Monfared, Max Monfared, Charlotte
Moore, Beth Shon, Meg Shon, William Slater,
Danielle Smale and Pippa Stannard.

*An explanation of difficult words can be
found in the glossary on page 31.*

THE SCIENCE OF
ELECTRICITY
& MAGNETISM

PROJECTS AND EXPERIMENTS
WITH ELECTRONS AND MAGNETS

STEVE PARKER

Heinemann
LIBRARY

CONTENTS

From microcircuits far too small to see...

...to powerful electric motors and magnets, to...

...coating things with shiny hard metal, the twin technologies of electricity and magnetism affect our daily life in endless ways.

INTRODUCTION

The world gets busier and more electromagnetic. Electricity lets us do many things, from making a phone call to cleaning our clothes. And wherever there is electricity, there is also magnetism. Electricity is our favourite form of energy. We can make it, we can transfer it from place to place easily, we can get it to carry information, and we can convert it to other forms of energy. All of these processes rely on our knowledge of the sciences of electricity and magnetism.

HOW IT WORKS

These panels explain the scientific ideas on which each project is based, and the processes that make it work.

Prepare each project carefully and follow the instructions. Remember: real scientists always put safety first.

WARNING

- Adults should oversee all experiments.
- All wires should be insulated.
- Don't ever touch a conductor when it is connected to an electrical current.
- Never connect the two terminals of a battery, or series of batteries, directly together.
- Do not experiment with a car battery.
- Never experiment with electrical sockets.

Where you see these symbols:

 Ask an adult to help you.

 Project to be done outdoors.

 Sharp tools may be needed.

Prepare work surface for a messy project.

1.5v battery   9v batteries

Batteries have a positive (+) terminal and a negative (–) terminal. You will need 1.5v and 9v batteries. Either type of 9v battery will do.

TRY IT AND SEE

These panels show further ideas for you to try, so that you can experiment and find out more about electricity and magnetism.

STATIC ELECTRICITY

Static electrical charge on a rubbed balloon pulls or attracts very light items which do not carry electric charge very well. They include bits of tissue paper, feathers, dust – and human hair.

Electricity is made by tiny particles called electrons. These are even smaller than the atoms which make up all substances and materials. In fact, electrons are inside atoms, whirling round and round. Electrons have electric charge. When they leave their atoms and set off on their own, they cause electricity.

In each atom, electrons go around the central part, called the nucleus.

PROJECT: MAKE A CAPACITOR (CHARGE-HOLDER)

CHARGE-HOLDER

WARNING! Do not charge the carrier more than about 10 times. Otherwise you might get a small shock!

WHAT YOU NEED

- polystyrene plate and cup
- camera film canister
- nail
- cooking foil
- wire
- foil tray

1

2

3

4

POUR WATER INTO A PLASTIC FILM CANISTER OR SIMILAR SMALL PLASTIC CONTAINER. FILL IT ABOUT TWO-THIRDS OF THE WAY UP AND FIRMLY CLIP ON THE LID.

WITH GREAT CARE ON A FIRM BASE, TAP A NAIL WITH A HAMMER SO THAT IT GOES THROUGH THE LID. MAKE SURE THE NAIL GOES DOWN FAR ENOUGH TO ENTER THE WATER.

FOLD SOME COOKING FOIL INTO A STRIP AND SMOOTH IT AROUND THE LOWER HALF OF THE CANISTER.

GLUE THE RIM OF A POLYSTYRENE CUP TO A FOIL TRAY. THIS IS THE CHARGE-CARRIER TO CONVEY ELECTRICAL CHARGE TO THE CANISTER, WHICH IS THE CAPACITOR.

STATIC TO MOVING

Rubbing the plate on the carpet makes atoms lose some of their electrons. Electrons have a negative charge, so the remaining atoms are positive. This positive charge transfers to the foil tray and then to the nail and water. The positive charges in the canister attract electrons as negative charges in the cooking foil. When the wire links the two, electrons rush along it from the foil into the nail, to even out the charges and restore the balance.

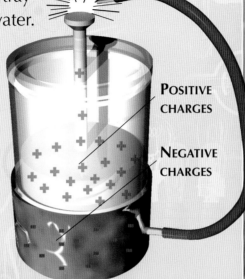

JUMPING ELECTRONS MAKE A SPARK

POSITIVE CHARGES

NEGATIVE CHARGES

MAGIC PULL

Rub materials like plastic, nylon, wool, and acrylic. See how the charges that build up on them attract small pieces of tissue paper.

TRY CHARGING A NYLON COMB WHEN IT IS DRY, THEN WET. DOES THE WATER LET THE CHARGE LEAK AWAY?

5

6

7

RUB A POLYSTYRENE PLATE BRISKLY FOR A FEW SECONDS ON A CARPET OR CLOTH MADE FROM WOOL OR NYLON. THE DRIER THE CONDITIONS, THE BETTER THIS PROJECT WILL WORK.

HOLD THE CHARGE-CARRIER BY THE CUP. TOUCH ITS FOIL TRAY ON TO THE POLYSTYRENE PLATE. THIS TRANSFERS THE ELECTRIC CHARGE FROM THE PLATE ON TO THE TRAY.

TOUCH THE FOIL TRAY TO THE NAIL SO THE CHARGE CAN ENTER THE CAPACITOR. REPEAT THE CHARGING PROCESS (5 AND 6) 10 TIMES TO INCREASE THE CHARGE IN THE CAPACITOR.

ZZZZAP

ATTACH A WIRE TO THE BASE. MAKE SURE YOU DO NOT TOUCH THE NAIL WHILE YOU DO THIS. HOLD THE WIRE AND GRADUALLY MOVE ITS END TO THE NAIL. EVENTUALLY THERE WILL BE A CRACK AS THE ELECTRONS JUMP. IF YOU DO THIS IN A DARK ROOM YOU SHOULD SEE A SPARK AS WELL.

HOW MUCH CHARGE?

In 1752 Benjamin Franklin flew a kite in a thunderstorm, to show that lightning was due to electric charge. The charge travelled down the damp string and caused a spark when it jumped from a key. Franklin was amazingly lucky, he could easily have been killed.

Until two hundred years ago, static charge was the only kind of electricity that scientists could use. It was stored in capacitors (then called Leyden jars), and it made cracks and sparks as it jumped from one substance to another. During experiments it was important to measure the amount of charge. In fact it still is, since many electrical devices today use modern types of capacitors.

PROJECT: MAKE A CHARGE MEASURER (ELECTROSCOPE)

CHARGE MEASURER

WHAT YOU NEED

- glass jar with plastic lid
- thick stiff wire (e.g. coat-hanger wire)
- cooking foil
- modelling clay
- balloon
- hammer
- nail
- wire cutters

1

TAKE THE LID OFF THE GLASS JAR. MAKE A SMALL HOLE IN THE CENTRE OF THE LID WITH A HAMMER AND NAIL, JUST WIDE ENOUGH FOR THE THICK METAL WIRE TO PASS THROUGH.

2

CUT OFF A SHORT LENGTH OF THE THICK, STIFF WIRE. BEND THE END AT A RIGHT ANGLE TO FORM AN L SHAPE. PUSH THE WIRE THROUGH THE LID HOLE AND FIX IT FIRMLY WITH MODELLING CLAY.

3

BEND A STRIP OF COOKING FOIL OVER THE LOWER END OF THE WIRE, LIKE A THIN UPSIDE-DOWN V. ROLL MORE FOIL INTO A TIGHT BALL. PUSH THIS ON TO THE UPPER END OF THE WIRE.

PUSH-PULL

Different charges attract one another. The same charges repel one another. Positive charges on the balloon attract negative ones up the wire to the ball, leaving positive charges on the foil strip. The positive charges on the strip's sides repel each other and make the sides push apart.

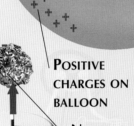

POSITIVE CHARGES ON BALLOON

NEGATIVE CHARGES ON BALL

POSITIVE CHARGES PUSH APART

PUSHED APART

BLOW UP A BALLOON AND RUB IT ON WOOL OR NYLON MATERIAL, SO ELECTRIC CHARGE OR STATIC COLLECTS ON ITS SURFACE. BRING THE BALLOON NEAR TO THE FOIL BALL, BUT WITHOUT TOUCHING. WATCH THE FOIL STRIP – ITS SIDES MOVE FARTHER APART! MOVE THE BALLOON AWAY AND THE STRIPS COME CLOSER TOGETHER AGAIN.

MEASURE

The greater the charge, the farther the strip's sides push apart. Charge used to be measured this way.

TRY USING THE CHARGED CAPACITOR FROM PAGE 6.

4

PUT THE LID BACK ON TO THE JAR. THE FOIL STRIP INSIDE SHOULD HANG DOWN FREELY WITH ONLY A VERY NARROW GAP BETWEEN THE TWO SIDES OF ITS V SHAPE.

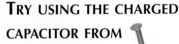

CIRCUITS AND SWITCHES

In static electricity, electrons stay still. In current electricity, as from a battery, the electrons flow steadily. But they must have a pathway or circuit made of a suitable substance to flow along. Substances that carry electricity well, mainly metals, are called electrical conductors.

In a complex circuit the electricity can flow along hundreds of different pathways.

PROJECT: MAKE A CIRCUIT WITH TWO-WAY SWITCHES

WHAT YOU NEED

- stiff card
- paper
- two 1.5-volt batteries
- 3-volt bulb in holder
- cooking foil
- wire
- pins

DRAW PICTURES ON PAPER OF THE UPSTAIRS, STAIRS, AND DOWNSTAIRS OF A HOUSE.

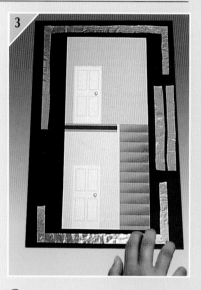

GLUE THE PICTURES ON TO THE CARD, WITH SPACE AROUND FOR THE CONDUCTORS.

CUT A CARD CIRCLE WITH A SIDE-TAB AND GLUE THE SAME SHAPE OF FOIL TO ONE SIDE, AS A SWITCH. MAKE ANOTHER AND FIT THEM FOIL-DOWN WITH PINS.

GLUE THE BULB-HOLDER TO THE CARD. POSITION THE BATTERIES SO THEY TOUCH + TO −−. RUN A WIRE FROM THE LOWER BATTERY TO THE LOWER FOIL STRIP, ONE FROM THE UPPER BATTERY TO ONE BULB CONTACT, AND ONE FROM THE OTHER BULB CONTACT TO THE UPPER STRIP.

CUT LONG STRIPS OF METAL FOIL AS CONDUCTORS AND GLUE THEM TO THE BOARD AS SHOWN.

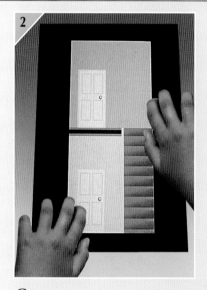

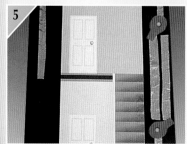

UPSTAIRS, DOWNSTAIRS

A SWITCH BREAKS THE CIRCUIT OF CONDUCTORS BY PUTTING AN AIR GAP INTO IT – AND AIR IS A VERY POOR CONDUCTOR. A ONE-WAY SWITCH IS EITHER ON, ALLOWING ELECTRICITY TO FLOW, OR OFF, STOPPING THE FLOW. IN THIS TWO-SWITCH CIRCUIT, EACH SWITCH CONTROLS THE FLOW.

THE LIGHT IS ON (BELOW LEFT) AS ELECTRICITY FLOWS THROUGH THE LEFT-HAND FOIL STRIP. IF YOU FLICK THE DOWNSTAIRS SWITCH...

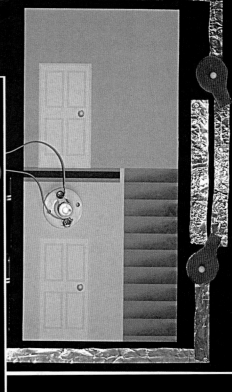

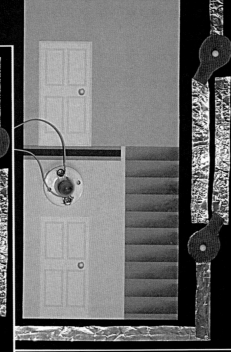

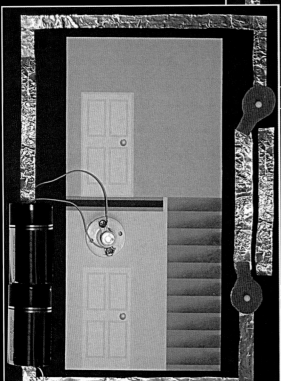

...THE CIRCUIT IS BROKEN BECAUSE THERE IS NO CONNECTION BETWEEN THE TWO FOIL STRIPS. SO THE LIGHT GOES OUT (ABOVE). THEN LATER...

...WHEN YOU ARE UPSTAIRS, YOU MIGHT WANT TO TURN THE LIGHT ON. FLICKING THE UPSTAIRS SWITCH MAKES A COMPLETE CIRCUIT AGAIN BECAUSE ELECTRICITY CAN NOW FLOW THROUGH THE RIGHT-HAND FOIL STRIP (ABOVE). SO THE BULB GLOWS AGAIN. THIS WORKS TIME, AFTER TIME, AFTER TIME...

FLOWING CHARGES

If an electron is given enough 'push', it leaves its atom and looks for another atom which lacks an electron. A battery provides enough 'push' for all the electrons to do this along a metal wire.

As a result, billions of electrons all do the same, hopping from one atom to the next in the same direction along the wire. This flow of charges or electrons is called an electric current.

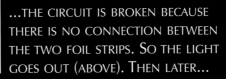

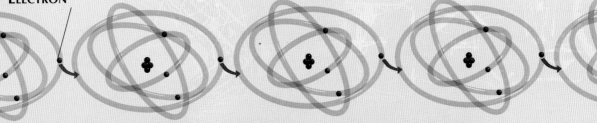

ATOM   ELECTRON

NUCLEUS

FLOW OR NO FLOW?

In high-power electricity cables, the insulators look like stacked discs made of special ceramic material.

Electricity does not flow out of plugs, sockets, and devices such as televisions, because air does not allow it. Substances that carry electricity are conductors; those which do not are called insulators. Electrical wires are made to be good conductors. Air is a good insulator. What about other everyday substances and materials?

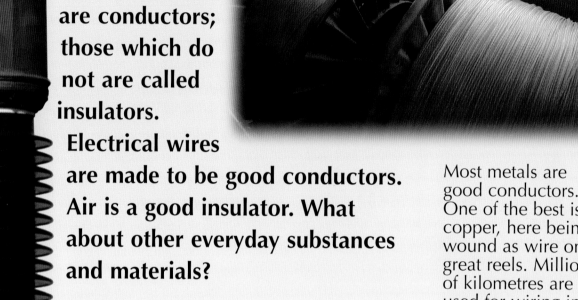

Most metals are good conductors. One of the best is copper, here being wound as wire on to great reels. Millions of kilometres are used for wiring in buildings and electrical machines.

PROJECT: BUILD A CONDUCTION TESTER

CONDUCTION TESTER

WHAT YOU NEED

- electrical wires
- pins
- 3-volt bulb in holder
- 1.5-volt battery
- polyboard
- tape

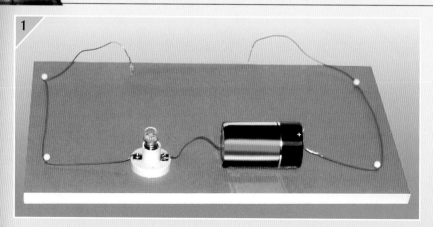

TAPE A BATTERY AND A BULB IN ITS HOLDER TO THE POLYBOARD BASE. CONNECT ONE BULB CONTACT TO ONE END OF THE BATTERY WITH WIRE. ATTACH LONGER WIRES TO THE OTHER END OF THE BATTERY AND THE OTHER BULB CONTACT, AND PIN AS SHOWN.

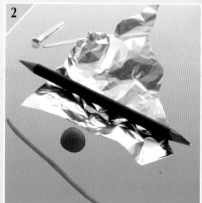

COLLECT A WIDE RANGE OF EVERYDAY OBJECTS MADE OF DIFFERENT MATERIALS TO TEST. WILL THEY CONDUCT OR NOT?

BRIDGING THE GAP

Electricity only flows when it has a complete pathway or circuit of conductors. If a conductor bridges the gap between the wire ends, electrons move and make the bulb light. Insulating materials prevent this.

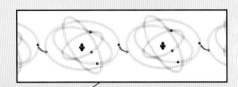

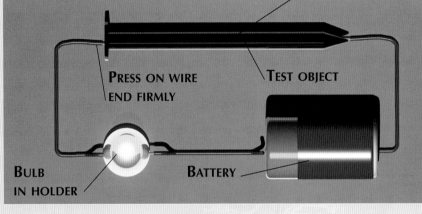

PRESS ON WIRE END FIRMLY

TEST OBJECT

BULB IN HOLDER

BATTERY

SEMI-FLOW?

Put the 'lead' of a pencil, which is really the substance graphite, across the gap. The bulb may glow slightly. Graphite is a weak conductor and lets through some electricity but not all.

TRY PENCILS OF DIFFERENT LENGTHS. IS THERE A BRIGHTER GLOW WITH A SHORTER PENCIL? WHAT ABOUT THE WOOD OF THE PENCIL?

GLOW OR NO GLOW?
TO TEST A MATERIAL, PLACE THE OBJECT IN THE GAP BETWEEN THE ENDS OF THE LONGER WIRES. HOLDING THE WIRES BY THEIR PLASTIC COVERINGS, PRESS THEIR BARE METAL ENDS ON TO THE OBJECT TO MAKE A GOOD CONNECTION. IF THE BULB GLOWS, THE MATERIAL IS A CONDUCTOR. IF NOT, IT'S AN INSULATOR.

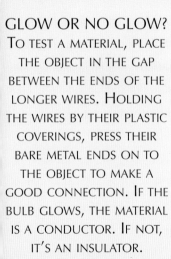

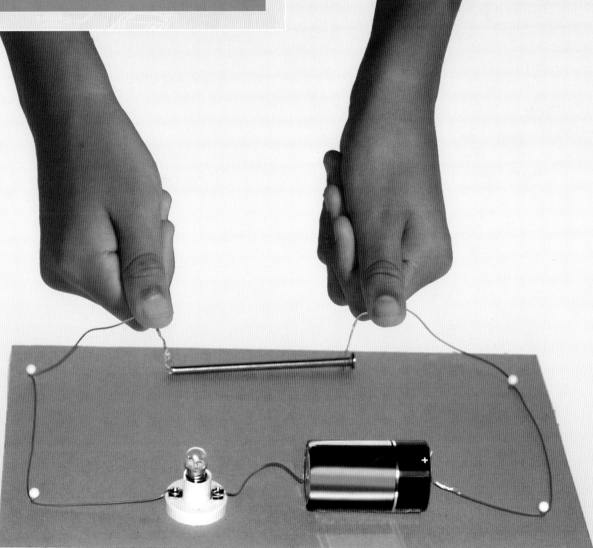

RESIST THE FLOW

Good insulators hold back or resist the flow of electricity. They have very high resistance. Good conductors have very low resistance and let electricity through. In some circuits and machines, there's a need to change the amount of resistance.

A dimmer switch alters the glow of a light bulb, from full brightness to almost none.

PROJECT: MAKE A DIMMER SWITCH

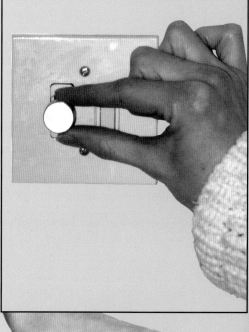

DIMMER SWITCH

WARNING!
Do not allow the bulb to shine for too long, especially dimly. Heat may build up in the wire coil.

WHAT YOU NEED

- **electrical wire**
- **sandpaper**
- **wooden block**
- **3-volt bulb in holder**
- **1.5-volt battery**
- **cardboard tube**
- **polyboard**
- **glue**

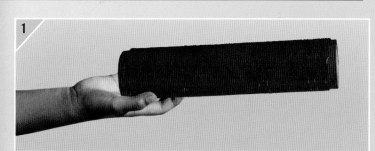

WIND A PIECE OF PLASTIC-COATED WIRE AROUND A LARGE CARD TUBE IN NEAT TURNS, SIDE BY SIDE. PUSH THE BARE ENDS INTO HOLES AT THE TUBE'S ENDS.

WRAP SANDPAPER AROUND A WOODEN BLOCK. USE IT TO RUB THE PLASTIC COATING FROM THE WIRE IN A LONG STRIP, TO LEAVE THE WIRE'S BARE METAL EXPOSED.

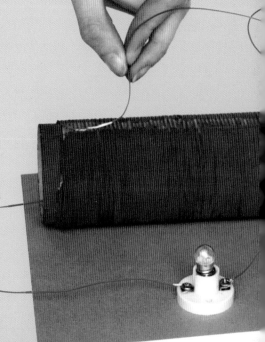

FIX THE BATTERY, THE BULB IN ITS HOLDER, AND THREE LENGTHS OF WIRE ON TO A POLYBOARD BASE, AS SHOWN FOR THE CONDUCTOR-TESTER ON THE LAST PAGE. JOIN ONE OF THE LONG WIRES TO THE WIRE AT ONE END OF THE TUBE.

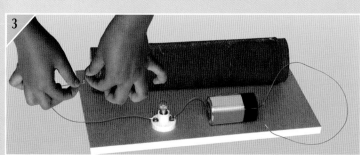

MORE = LESS

Even copper wire puts up a small resistance to electricity. The longer the wire, the greater this resistance, and so less electricity flows around the circuit. As you move the 'wiper' along the coil from left to right, electricity must flow through more turns. More wire means less electricity and so a dimmer bulb.

ELECTRICITY FLOWS THROUGH ONLY A SHORT PART OF THE COIL

ELECTRICITY FLOWS THROUGH A LONGER PART OF THE COIL

BRIGHTER AND DIMMER

THE FREE END OF THE LONG WIRE IS THE 'WIPER'. HOLD IT BY THE PLASTIC COVERING AND TOUCH IT TO THE BARE EXPOSED WIRE ON THE COIL. SLIDE IT TO AND FRO ALONG THE COIL, PRESSING TO KEEP A GOOD CONTACT. DOES THE BULB CHANGE BRIGHTNESS?

JUST AS DIM?

Obtain a bare length of pencil 'lead' or graphite (see previous page) as used in propelling pencils. Put this in place of the wire coil. Does the dimmer still work?

TRY MAKING THE COIL WITH THE TURNS FARTHER APART. THE BULB MAY GLOW BRIGHTER – BUT IS THE WIPER EASY TO USE?

ADD UP OR SHARE OUT?

A simple circuit has a battery and bulb connected by wires. Increasing the number of parts, or components, in a circuit also increases the number of different ways they can be connected. One way is components in series, so electricity flows through them one after the other. Another is in parallel (side by side), when electricity passes through them at the same time.

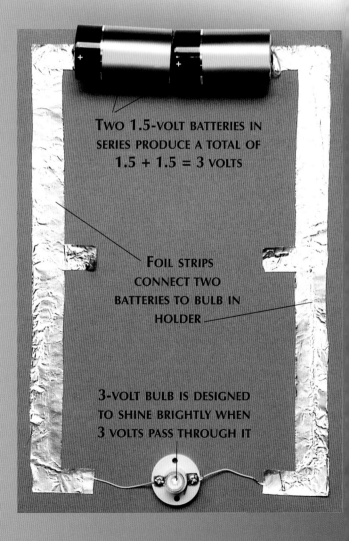

In a battery charger, the batteries are in parallel. Each one receives the full amount of charging electricity.

Torch batteries are in series, one behind the other. If they are both 1.5 volts, together they produce 3 volts.

PROJECT: TEST CIRCUIT DESIGNS

CIRCUIT DESIGN TESTER

WHAT YOU NEED

- **thick card**
- **glue**
- **cooking foil**
- **electrical wire**
- **two 1.5-volt batteries**
- **two 3-volt bulbs in holders**
- **tape**

MAKE A CIRCUIT BOARD FROM FOIL STRIPS GLUED TO A BASE (ABOVE). PREPARE LENGTHS OF ELECTRICAL WIRE TO LINK THE BATTERIES, BULBS, AND FOIL STRIPS IN VARIOUS WAYS.

BATTERIES IN SERIES

PLACE TWO BATTERIES INTO THE UPPER GAP, + OF ONE TOUCHING − OF THE OTHER. TAPE A WIRE FROM EACH REMAINING BATTERY CONTACT TO THE FOIL. CONNECT THE BULB INTO THE LOWER GAP. IS ITS GLOW BRIGHT?

TWO 1.5-VOLT BATTERIES IN SERIES PRODUCE A TOTAL OF 1.5 + 1.5 = 3 VOLTS

FOIL STRIPS CONNECT TWO BATTERIES TO BULB IN HOLDER

3-VOLT BULB IS DESIGNED TO SHINE BRIGHTLY WHEN 3 VOLTS PASS THROUGH IT

CIRCUITS AND SUMS

For two batteries joined in series, their 'pushing strength' in volts is twice as much. For batteries joined in parallel, the volts stay the same. However, the amount of electricity, which is the current measured in amps, is twice as much. If bulbs are joined in series the resistance of each one, measured in ohms, adds up.

If the batteries are joined in parallel, their resistances are 'shared' and so they are less. Scientists use a rule called Ohm's Law to work out the volts, amps, and ohms in a circuit, depending on the way components are joined.

BATTERIES IN PARALLEL

USE THE SAME CIRCUIT BOARD, CONNECT ONE BATTERY INTO THE UPPER GAP AND ONE INTO THE MIDDLE GAP. LEAVE THE BULB IN THE LOWER GAP. THE BULB NOW GLOWS LESS BRIGHTLY — BUT IF LEFT ON, IT WOULD SHINE FOR LONGER THAN WITH BATTERIES IN SERIES.

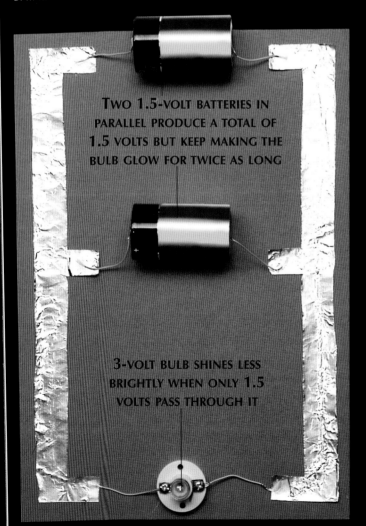

TWO 1.5-VOLT BATTERIES IN PARALLEL PRODUCE A TOTAL OF 1.5 VOLTS BUT KEEP MAKING THE BULB GLOW FOR TWICE AS LONG

3-VOLT BULB SHINES LESS BRIGHTLY WHEN ONLY 1.5 VOLTS PASS THROUGH IT

MORE DESIGNS

Try similar experiments to those on the left, but use only one battery. This time connect the bulbs in series and then parallel, as shown below. How do you think the bulbs will behave?

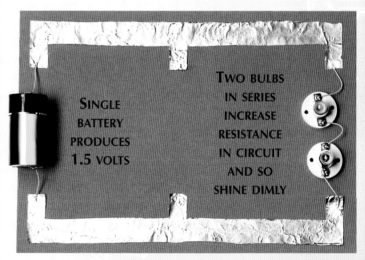

SINGLE BATTERY PRODUCES 1.5 VOLTS

TWO BULBS IN SERIES INCREASE RESISTANCE IN CIRCUIT AND SO SHINE DIMLY

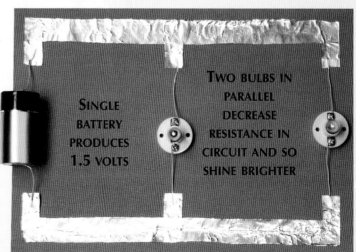

SINGLE BATTERY PRODUCES 1.5 VOLTS

TWO BULBS IN PARALLEL DECREASE RESISTANCE IN CIRCUIT AND SO SHINE BRIGHTER

MYSTERY MAGNETISM

Magnetism is a mysterious force. We cannot see it, but we can feel a magnet pull or push against other objects – especially other magnets. A magnet has 'opposite' poles, north or + and south or –.

PROJECT: MAKE A MAGLEV TRAIN

MAGLEV TRAIN

WHAT YOU NEED

- **plenty of small bar magnets**
- **thick card or polyboard**
- **glue**
- **scissors**
- **screwdriver**

1 GATHER 12 OR MORE SMALL BAR-SHAPED MAGNETS. IT MAY BE POSSIBLE TO 'BORROW' THEM TEMPORARILY FROM FRIDGE NOTE-HOLDERS OR MAGNETIC LETTERS, BY LEVERING THEM OUT GENTLY WITH A SCREWDRIVER.

2 GLUE THE MAGNETS TO THE TRACK – A LONG NARROW CARD STRIP. ENSURE THE SAME POLE OF EACH FACES UPWARD (SEE PANEL OPPOSITE).

3 CUT OUT TWO MORE LONG THIN STRIPS OF CARD. GLUE THEM TO THE EDGES OF THE TRACK TO GIVE IT SMOOTH SIDES.

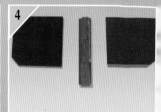

4 CUT OUT A CARD STRIP THREE MAGNETS LONG AND 2 MM WIDER THAN THE TRACK, FOR THE TRAIN. GLUE ON THE MAGNETS. ENSURE THE SAME POLES FACE DOWN AND THESE ARE THE SAME AS THE POLES FACING UP ON THE TRACK. CUT TWO CARD SIDES FOR THE TRAIN.

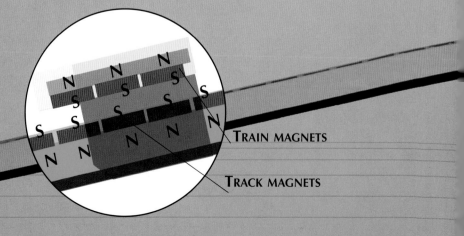

TRAIN MAGNETS

TRACK MAGNETS

'Maglev' means magnetic levitation (lifting). The train has no wheels. Magnetic forces make it 'float'.

LAW OF MAGNETISM

Like electric charges, magnetic poles show pulling or pushing forces. The basic law is that the same poles, such as north and north, or south and south, push apart. Different poles, north and south, pull together. The law is usually said: 'Like poles repel, unlike poles attract.'

UNLIKE POLES ATTRACT

LIKE POLES REPEL

5

GLUE THE SIDES ON TO THE TRAIN. CHECK IT FITS OVER THE TRACK — THE SIDES KEEP IT UPRIGHT. IF THE TRAIN CLAMPS DOWN HARD ON TO THE TRACK, ONE SET OF MAGNETS IS THE WRONG WAY ROUND!

6

MAKE A TOP FOR THE TRAIN BY CUTTING OUT THE PAPER SHAPE SHOWN ABOVE. FOLD IT ALONG THE DOTTED LINES AND GLUE THE OVERLAPPING FLAPS.

7

THE FINISHED TRAIN LOOKS SOMETHING LIKE THIS. MAKE THREE CARD STANDS TO SUPPORT THE TRACK AT AN ANGLE.

SILENT SLIDE
PLACE THE TRAIN AT THE TOP OF THE TRACK AND LET IT GO. IT SHOULD SLIDE DOWN SMOOTHLY AND QUIETLY. THE POLES OF THE TRACK AND TRAIN MAGNETS REPEL TO MAKE THE TRAIN 'HOVER'.

DIFFERENT SHAPES

All magnets have a north and a south pole.

TO FIND THE POLES, HOLD A PAIR OF MAGNETS TOGETHER AND FEEL WHERE THE FORCES ARE STRONGEST.

MAGNETIC WORLD

Magnetism affects mainly iron-containing substances. The centre or core of the Earth is very hot iron, which makes our whole planet into a giant magnet. This is why the names North and South Pole apply both to magnets and to the entire Earth. We use a much smaller magnet to detect Earth's magnetic forces, using the basic law of magnetism from the previous page.

A compass is vital for walkers, sailors, explorers, pilots, and others on long journeys.

PROJECT: MAKE A COMPASS

COMPASS

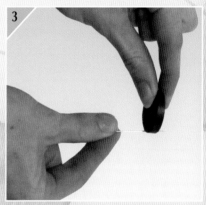

DRAW A CIRCLE 2 CM SMALLER THAN THE JAR LID AND CUT IT OUT. COLOUR A PATTERN ON IT WITH A BLACK ARROW.

CUT A LARGE SQUARE OF CLEAR STICKY-BACKED PLASTIC. SMOOTH IT OVER THE COLOURED SIDE OF THE PAPER CIRCLE.

STROKE THE NEEDLE IN THE SAME DIRECTION WITH THE SAME POLE OF A MAGNET, OVER 300 TIMES. IT BECOMES A MAGNET TOO.

WHAT YOU NEED

- **paper**
- **steel sewing needle**
- **magnet**
- **plastic jar lid**
- **clear sticky-back plastic**
- **scissors**
- **coloured pens or paints**

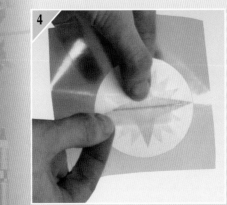

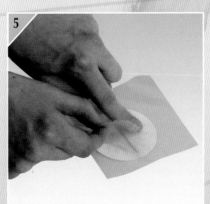

TEST THE NEEDLE'S N AND S POLES (PAGE 19). TAPE IT WITH ITS N UNDER THE BLACK ARROW.

APPLY ANOTHER SQUARE OF STICKY-BACKED PLASTIC OVER THE NEEDLE AND CIRCLE, AS A SEAL.

TRIM THE PLASTIC ROUND THE CIRCLE, LEAVING 5 MM EXTRA AS A CLEAR EDGE ALL AROUND.

MAGNETIC FIELD

A magnet's forces are like lines between the poles, called lines of magnetic force. Earth's lines of force go from the North to South Pole. Held level, the compass needle's poles are attracted by the Earth's poles and point to them. At Earth's poles the lines of force enter the ground almost at right angles, but around Earth's middle they are parallel with the ground. Put a compass on its side pointing North and South, and its needle shows this angle, called dip or inclination. The whole area of magnetism is the magnetic field.

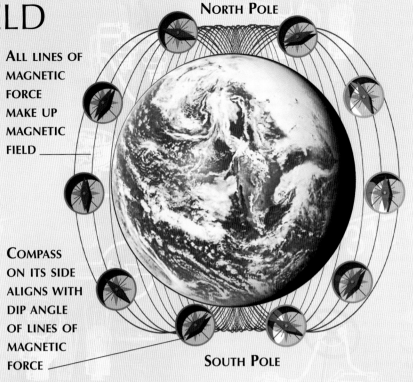

NORTH POLE

ALL LINES OF MAGNETIC FORCE MAKE UP MAGNETIC FIELD

COMPASS ON ITS SIDE ALIGNS WITH DIP ANGLE OF LINES OF MAGNETIC FORCE

SOUTH POLE

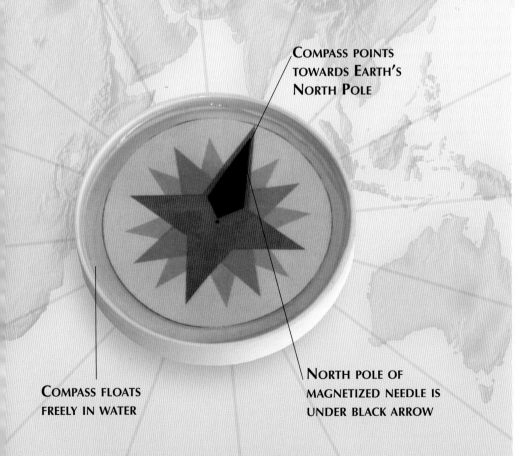

COMPASS POINTS TOWARDS EARTH'S NORTH POLE

COMPASS FLOATS FREELY IN WATER

NORTH POLE OF MAGNETIZED NEEDLE IS UNDER BLACK ARROW

WHICH WAY IS NORTH?
PUT SOME WATER IN THE JAR TOP. PLACE YOUR COMPASS IN THE WATER AND WATCH AS IT TURNS TO FACE NORTH. IF YOU USE IT OUTSIDE PUT THE GLASS JAR OVER THE TOP. THIS WILL STOP THE WIND AFFECTING IT.

SEE IT!

You can show a magnet's lines of force by placing the magnet under thin paper. Sprinkle iron filings on the paper and tap gently. What do you see?

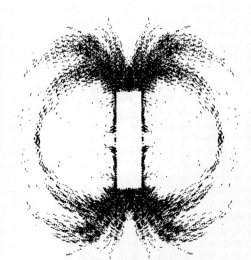

TRY THIS WITH DIFFERENT SHAPES OF MAGNETS, LIKE BUTTONS, HORSESHOES (U), AND RINGS.

ELECTRICAL MAGNETS

Electricity and magnetism are 'twins'. Almost always they occur together, as one of the most basic or fundamental forces in the universe – electromagnetism. When electricity flows, it makes a magnetic field around itself. If the electricity stops, the field stops. Electromagnets make great use of this on/off magnetism.

PROJECT: MAKE AN ELECTROMAGNET

Electromagnets are used in scrapyards to lift many tonnes.

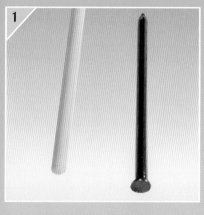

1 TRIM THE STRAW TO BE SLIGHTLY LONGER THAN THE NAIL. INSERT THE NAIL INTO THE STRAW.

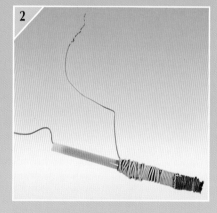

2 THREAD THE WIRE THROUGH THE STRAW TOO. WIND IT TO MAKE A HALF-COIL WITH FREE ENDS.

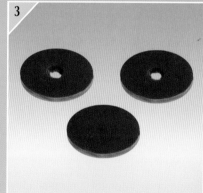

3 CUT THREE CARD CIRCLES THAT JUST FIT INTO THE TUBE. MAKE HOLES IN TWO WITH A PENCIL.

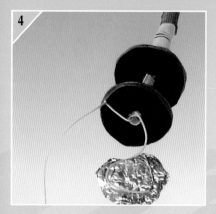

4 SLIDE THE HOLED CARD CIRCLES OVER THE STRAW. TAPE ONE WIRE END TO A PIECE OF FOIL AND GLUE THIS TO THE END CARD.

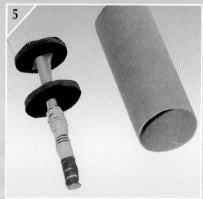

5 SLIDE THE ASSEMBLY OF CARD CIRCLES, NAIL, STRAW, AND WIRE COIL INTO THE TUBE. THE COIL PART STICKS OUT OF ONE END.

6 PUT A BATTERY IN THE TUBE, ONE CONTACT TOUCHING THE FOIL. THE WIRE SHOULD RUN PAST THE BATTERY TO ITS OTHER END.

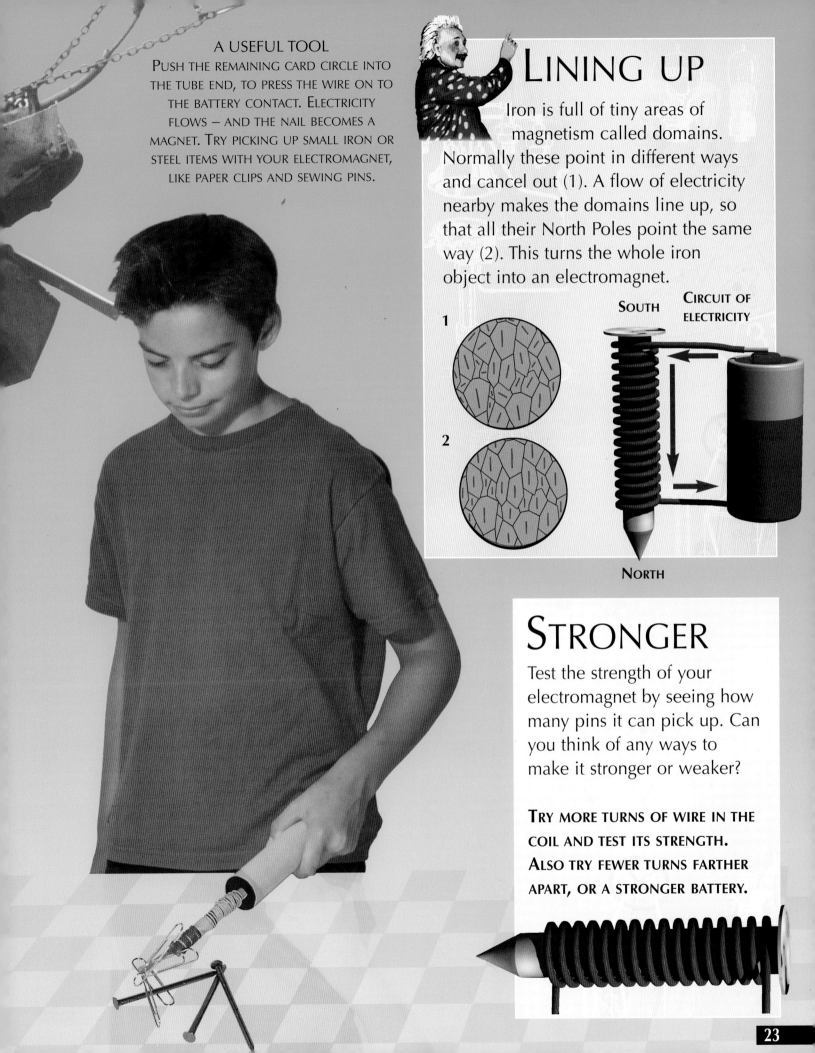

A USEFUL TOOL

Push the remaining card circle into the tube end, to press the wire on to the battery contact. Electricity flows – and the nail becomes a magnet. Try picking up small iron or steel items with your electromagnet, like paper clips and sewing pins.

LINING UP

Iron is full of tiny areas of magnetism called domains. Normally these point in different ways and cancel out (1). A flow of electricity nearby makes the domains line up, so that all their North Poles point the same way (2). This turns the whole iron object into an electromagnet.

SOUTH

CIRCUIT OF ELECTRICITY

1

2

NORTH

STRONGER

Test the strength of your electromagnet by seeing how many pins it can pick up. Can you think of any ways to make it stronger or weaker?

TRY MORE TURNS OF WIRE IN THE COIL AND TEST ITS STRENGTH. ALSO TRY FEWER TURNS FARTHER APART, OR A STRONGER BATTERY.

23

A car's central locking uses a two-way solenoid in each door to lock or unlock.

ELECTRO-PULL

Electromagnets can be used to make movements. A typical electromagnet has a coil of wire wrapped around an iron rod, the core, that does not move. A solenoid is an electromagnet with a core that can move. If the core is not fully inside the coil when the electricity switches on, it is pulled inside.

PROJECT: MAKE A SOLENOID LOCK

A loudspeaker moves to and fro due to magnetic forces on the coil of wire at the back.

SOLENOID LOCK

WARNING! Solenoids, being similar to electromagnets, may become hot if they are left on for too long. Do not let the electricity flow for more than a few seconds.

WHAT YOU NEED

- straw
- paper clips
- electrical wire
- 9-volt battery
- thick card or polyboard
- glue
- scissors
- pencil
- insulating tape

1

CUT OUT THREE 25 MM SQUARES OF THICK CARD OR POLYBOARD. MAKE A STRAW-SIZED HOLE IN THE MIDDLE OF TWO OF THEM USING A PENCIL.

2

CUT A 15 MM LENGTH OF STRAW. GLUE IT UPRIGHT TO THE THIRD SQUARE.

3

4

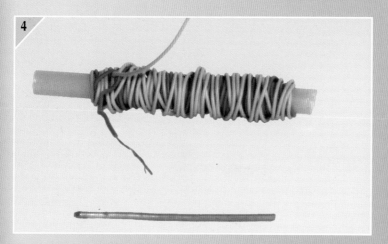

TRIM A PIECE OF STRAW 1 CM GREATER THAN THE LENGTH OF THE SOLENOID. COIL THE WIRE MANY TIMES AROUND THE STRAW, LEAVING LONG FREE ENDS. STRAIGHTEN A PAPER CLIP TO MAKE THE INNER ROD OR CORE.

CUT OUT A BASE ABOUT 12 CM SQUARE AND AN UPRIGHT STAND ABOUT 8 CM BY 15 CM. CUT A SLOT IN THE MIDDLE OF THE BASE JUST BIG ENOUGH FOR THE BOTTOM EDGE OF THE STAND. GLUE THE STAND INTO THE SLOT. GLUE THE THREE SQUARES TO THE STAND, PROJECTING FORWARD LIKE SHELVES AS SHOWN. THE DISTANCE BETWEEN THE TOP AND MIDDLE SQUARES WILL BE THE LENGTH OF THE SOLENOID.

PULLED TO THE CENTRE

When electricity flows along a straight wire, the magnetism around the wire is very weak. In a wire coil, the magnetism around all the turns adds together to produce a much stronger force. The magnetism in an electromagnet is exactly the same as in an ordinary or permanent magnet. It attracts nearby objects made of iron. The paper clip core is steel, which consists mainly of iron. So the core is pulled forcefully into the centre of the magnetic field.

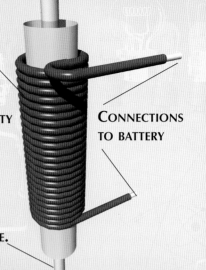

SOLENOID COIL MAKES A MAGNETIC FIELD WHEN ELECTRICITY FLOWS.

CONNECTIONS TO BATTERY

SOLENOID CORE IS PULLED INTO COIL BY MAGNETIC FORCE.

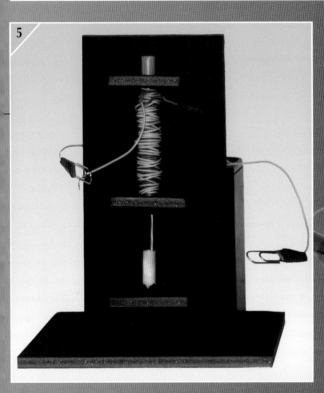

5

FIT THE STRAW INTO THE HOLES IN THE UPPER AND LOWER SQUARES. DROP THE PAPER CLIP DOWN THE STRAW TO REST IN THE LOWER STRAW. CONNECT TWO PAPER CLIPS WITH INSULATING TAPE TO TWO PIECES OF WIRE THAT ARE ATTACHED TO THE BATTERY TERMINALS.

LOCK ...UNLOCK ... LOCK ...

WHEN YOU CONNECT THE PAPER CLIPS TO THE WIRES FROM THE COIL, ELECTRICITY FLOWS AND MAKES A MAGNETIC FIELD. THIS PULLS THE CORE UP INTO THE MIDDLE OF THE COIL AND 'UNLOCKS' THE LOWER STRAW. WHEN THE ELECTRICITY STOPS, GRAVITY PULLS THE CORE BACK DOWN AND 'LOCKS' THE STRAW AGAIN.

MOTOR POWER

Car-sized motors in electric trains move hundreds of tonnes of carriages, passengers, and cargoes.

Electricity and magnetism are combined to make a spinning motion in one of the world's most useful gadgets – the electric motor. Some motors are smaller than pinheads. Others are bigger than trucks. But they all depend on split-second timing to switch on electricity – and magnetism.

Most electric motors have many sets of windings, to give a smooth and powerful turning action.

PROJECT: MAKE AN ELECTRIC MOTOR

ELECTRIC MOTOR

WARNING!
The wire must be thin but stiff and have a thin covering or coating of insulation. Be especially careful in stage 4, removing part of this coating.

WHAT YOU NEED

- thin coated electrical wire
- two large paper clips
- disc magnet
- 9-volt battery
- thick card or polyboard
- glue
- knife

1

CUT A CARD OR BOARD BASE AND UPRIGHT STAND EACH ABOUT 20 CM LONG. GLUE THE STAND ON TO THE BASE.

2

STRAIGHTEN EACH LARGE PAPER CLIP AND BEND A DEEP HOOK AT ONE END.

3

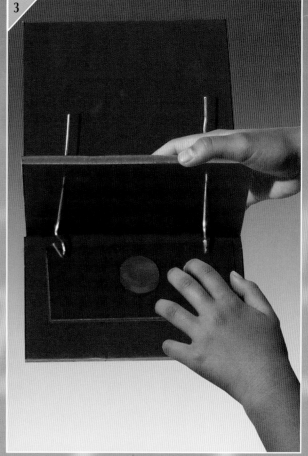

4

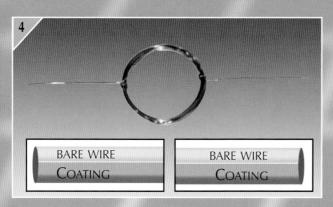

| BARE WIRE | | BARE WIRE | |
| COATING | | COATING | |

WIND THE WIRE INTO A 6 CM CIRCULAR COIL, WITH TWO LONG ENDS STICKING OUT AT OPPOSITE SIDES. WITH A BLUNT KNIFE, CAREFULLY SCRAPE AWAY THE INSULATING COATING ON THE UPPER SIDE OF EACH WIRE ONLY (SEE ALSO DIAGRAM IN PANEL OPPOSITE).

MAKE TWO SMALL HOLES AT THE SAME HEIGHT IN THE CENTRE PANEL. PUSH THE PAPER CLIPS THROUGH. PLACE A DISC OR BUTTON MAGNET ON A PIECE OF THICK BOARD. POSITION IT ON THE BASE, MIDWAY BETWEEN THE PAPER CLIP HOOKS.

PUSH-AROUND

Electricity passing through the coil of wire makes it into an electromagnet. Its magnetic field pushes or pulls against the field of the permanent disc magnet, making the coil move and turn. But after a short distance the electricity stops since the wire coating now touches the paper clip and no electricity can pass. However, the coil's spinning motion carries it around further, until the bare wire again touches the paper clip, electricity flows, and...

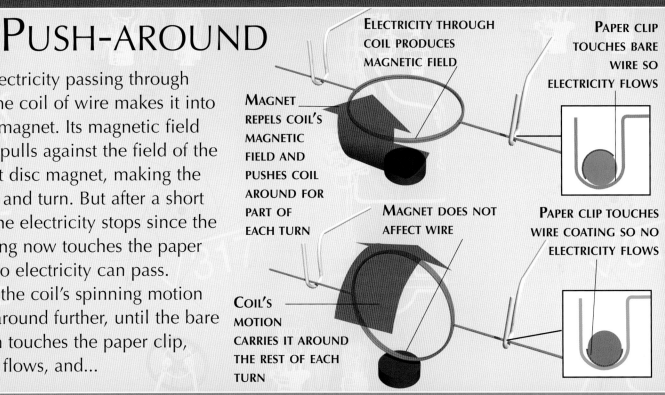

ELECTRICITY THROUGH COIL PRODUCES MAGNETIC FIELD

PAPER CLIP TOUCHES BARE WIRE SO ELECTRICITY FLOWS

MAGNET REPELS COIL'S MAGNETIC FIELD AND PUSHES COIL AROUND FOR PART OF EACH TURN

MAGNET DOES NOT AFFECT WIRE

PAPER CLIP TOUCHES WIRE COATING SO NO ELECTRICITY FLOWS

COIL'S MOTION CARRIES IT AROUND THE REST OF EACH TURN

5

Hang the wire coil centrally on the paper clip hooks. Make sure that as it rotates it comes very near the magnet, but does not actually touch it. Add more layers of card under the magnet as necessary, to adjust its height.

Make connectors out of ordinary wire and paper clips between the coil and battery.

6

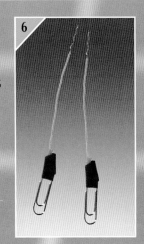

IN A SPIN

Connect the battery to the large paper clips. Give the wire coil a starting push — and it should spin on its own. For best results you may have to adjust the magnet's position and re-check the removal of the wire's insulating coating.

9V - PP9 - 6F100

ELECTRO-SPLIT

Electricity flows very well through water. This is why it's so important never to touch electrical gadgets and appliances with wet hands or in damp conditions. Electricity also has an effect on water itself. It can make substances dissolved in the water move about – sometimes with very useful results.

Items of solid silver are very costly. Electro-plating silver on to cheaper metals makes them look expensive.

Car wheels can be electroplated with the very hard, shiny metal called chromium. This chrome-plating does not rust, and its shine lasts longer.

PROJECT: ELECTROPLATE A NAIL WITH COPPER

ELECTROPLATING

WARNING! Do this project in a well-ventilated area, as fumes are given off.

WHAT YOU NEED

- electrical wire
- paper clips
- large nail
- 9-volt battery
- vinegar
- thick card
- glass jar
- glue
- bare copper wire
- tape
- salt

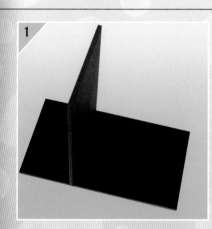

1. CUT A BASE AND STAND 20 CM BY 12 CM FROM CARD. GLUE THE STAND ON TO THE BASE.

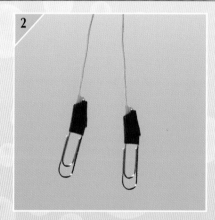

2. MAKE TWO CONNECTORS OF WIRE AND PAPER CLIPS, TO LINK THE BATTERY TO THE ELECTRODES.

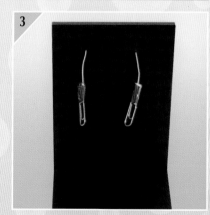

3. MAKE TWO HOLES IN THE UPPER STAND AND THREAD THROUGH THE WIRE CONNECTORS.

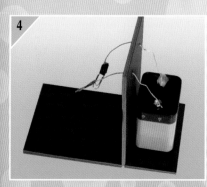

4. ATTACH THE CONNECTORS TO THE BATTERY BEHIND THE STAND.

5. PUSH THE NAIL AND PIECE OF COPPER WIRE THROUGH A STRIP OF CARD LONG ENOUGH TO FIT OVER THE GLASS OR JAR, AS SHOWN.

ELECTROLYSIS

Electricity passes through a liquid like water or vinegar between two contacts, or electrodes. When it does so it can cause chemical reactions. This is called electrolysis. The electricity in the liquid makes positive ions at the copper electrode. These have a positive electric charge. The positive ions are attracted to the negative electrode, the nail.

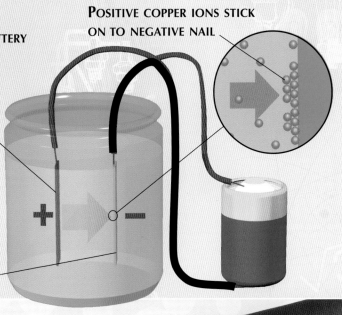

POSITIVE COPPER IONS STICK ON TO NEGATIVE NAIL

POSITIVE BATTERY TERMINAL CONNECTED TO COPPER WIRE ELECTRODE

NEGATIVE BATTERY TERMINAL CONNECTED TO NAIL ELECTRODE

POUR THE VINEGAR INTO THE GLASS. ADD SOME SALT AND STIR WELL. PLACE THE CARD STRIP WITH THE NAIL AND COPPER WIRE OVER THE TOP. CONNECT THE BATTERY'S + TO THE COPPER AND ITS − TO THE NAIL.

COPPER NAIL?
AFTER AN HOUR OR TWO, DISCONNECT THE BATTERY AND LIFT OUT THE NAIL. IT SHOULD BE COVERED WITH A GOLDEN-RED LAYER WHERE IT HAS BEEN IN THE VINEGAR. THIS IS COPPER PLATING MADE BY THE PROCESS OF ELECTROLYSIS.

LOOK AROUND

Using electricity to cover an item with a thin layer of another substance, usually a metal, is known as electroplating. It's a common way of protecting materials like steel, that tend to tarnish, corrode or go rusty.

ELECTRIC HISTORY

2,600 years ago Thales of Ancient Greece saw that rubbing a piece of amber made it attract lightweight objects such as feathers. This was due to the pulling force of electrostatic charge (static electricity). But for centuries the attracting powers of electrical charges and magnetic fields were greatly confused.

1600 William Gilbert's book suggested that the Earth is a huge magnet. He invented the name 'electricity'.

1729 Stephen Gray discovered that electricity (as static charge) was on the outside of an object, not inside. He noted that electrical charges were carried or transmitted by certain substances but not others, beginning the idea of conductors and insulators.

1751 Benjamin Franklin described electricity as an invisible fluid and showed that it could make a needle into a magnet. The next year he carried out his dangerous kite experiment, to show that lightning is a form of electrical discharge.

1773 Charles Dufay found that two rubbed pieces of amber repelled each other. He said that electricity was two sorts of fluid, depending on which substance was rubbed.

1786 Luigi Galvani noticed that a dead frog's legs twitched when touched with certain metals. He had the idea that 'animal electricity' was made in living things.

1800 Alessandro Volta made a set of electrical cells, the 'voltaic pile' – now called a battery.

1820 Hans Christian Oersted showed that a wire carrying electricity makes a magnetic field around it and affects a compass.

1820s Andre-Marie Ampère made many advances in electricity and electromagnetism, while William Sturgeon and Joseph Henry developed electromagnets.

1830s Michael Faraday devised early forms of electric generators and motors.

The first telegraphs used electricity to send messages long-distances.

1867 James Clerk Maxwell showed that electricity and magnetism were part of the same force, electromagnetism, and that light rays are waves of this force.

1904 John Ambrose Fleming invented the 'vacuum tube' or valve, helping to start the science of electronics.

GLOSSARY

Amperes (amps) Unit for measuring the amount of flow, or current, of electricity – the number of electrons going past per second.

Atom The smallest piece or particle of a pure substance (chemical element). Two or more atoms joined together form a molecule.

Battery A device that makes a flow of electricity from the chemicals inside. One 'battery' on its own is really an electrical cell, while a true 'battery' is lots of cells joined together.

Capacitor Device for storing electrical charge, sometimes called a condenser (formerly a Leyden jar).

Charge The electron has a negative charge. The rest of the atom has a positive charge. Negative charge is shown by a minus sign (–) and positive charge is shown by a plus sign (+).

Conductor A substance or material that carries electricity really well.

Current The flow of electricity through a circuit of conductors.

Electromagnet Magnetic forces produced by the flow of electricity through a conductor (usually a coil of wire).

Electrons Particles which are parts of atoms – they swirl round and round the central part, or nucleus, of the atom.

Insulator A substance or material that greatly resists the flow of electricity.

Magnetic field The area around a magnet where its magnetic force acts or is felt.

Ohms Unit for measuring the opposition or resistance of a substance to the flow of electricity.

Pole In magnetism, one of two places in a magnet where the magnetic forces are strongest or most concentrated.

Static electricity The effects produced between electric charges which don't move.

Volts Unit for measuring the 'pushing strength' of electricity, known as the potential difference (pd) or electromotive force (emf).

INDEX